Park Beat

Rhymin' Through the Seasons

By Jonathan London

Illustrated by Woodleigh Marx Hubbard

HarperCollins Publishers

Park Beat
Text copyright © 2001 by Jonathan London
Illustrations copyright © 2001 by Woodleigh Marx Hubbard
Printed in Hong Kong All rights reserved.
www.harperchildrens.com

Library of Congress Cataloging-in-Publication Data
London, Jonathan.
    Park beat / by Jonathan London ; illustrated by Woodleigh Marx Hubbard.
        p.   cm.
    Summary: Rhyming text describes activities and sights during the four seasons.
    ISBN 0-688-13994-9 (trade). — ISBN 0-688-13995-7 (lib. bdg.)
    [1. Seasons—Fiction.   2. Stories in rhyme.]   I. Hubbard, Woodleigh, ill.   II. Title.
PZ8.3.L8433Wal   2000   99-27643
[E]—dc21   CIP
                                                                                                 AC

Typography by Robbin Gourley
2   3   4   5   6   7   8   9   10
❖

For all our all-seasons walkin'-and-talkin' friends, Bob & Pat & Leah,
Michelle & Christine, & Gerard, with thanks to Sean —J.L.

In joyful and loving memory of Coriander 8 and Blake 6 —W.M.H.

The illustrator would like to express gratitude to Melanie Donovan,
Golda Laurens, and Andrea Brown; with special huzzahs for my wildly
supportive friends, Katrina and Isa.

Dogs yappin' and geese flappin',
Fish jumpin' and apples thumpin',

Squirrels blatherin' and nut-gatherin',

**Gardeners reapin' and cornstalks heapin',
Branches rattlin' and fires cracklin',**

**Pumpkins grinnin' and spiders spinnin',
Wind howlin' and goblins prowlin',**

Pies bakin' and Papa's rakin',

Leaves fallin' and Mama's callin',

I'm runnin' and flyin'—_wheeee! crash!_
And now I'm lyin' in a pile of leaves,

Rappin' and tappin' and finger-snappin'
On a walk through fall.

Breath steamin' and icicles gleamin',
Scarves blowin' and candles glowin',

Mittens missin' and skaters kissin',

**Sleigh bells jinglin' and fingers tinglin',
Sleds slidin' and some collidin',**

Kids shakin' and angel-makin',

Papa's plowin' and dog's bowwowin',

Snow's fallin' and Mama's callin',

Snowballs flyin'—*zing! oof!*
And now I'm lyin' in a pile of snow,

Rappin' and tappin' and finger-snappin'
On a walk through winter.

**Birds chirpin' and frogs burpin',
Creek's flowin' and flowers growin',**

**Crickets bouncin' and kittens pouncin',
Gardeners putterin' and butterflies flutterin',**

Clouds bloomin' and storm's loomin',

Rain's fallin' and Mama's callin',

I'm slippin' and slidin'—*oops! yikes!*
And now I'm glidin' in a puddle of mud,

**Rappin' and tappin' and finger-snappin'
On a walk through spring.**

Ducks cruisin' and turtles snoozin',
Flickers drummin' and honeybees hummin',

Kids berry-pickin' and ice-cream-lickin',

**Ballplayers sweatin' and hot sun's settin',
Sprinklers sprinklin' and wind chimes tinklin',**

Hot dogs roastin' and skaters coastin',

Papa's loungin' and dog's scroungin',

Night's fallin' and Mama's callin',

Fireflies flashin'—*wheeee! smack!* And now I'm splashin' in our backyard pool, Rappin' and tappin' and finger-snappin' on a walk through summer.